FIND ✦ DISCOVER ✦ LEARN

BIG BOOK OF MY BODY

CLEVER
• Publishing •

PARTS OF YOUR BODY

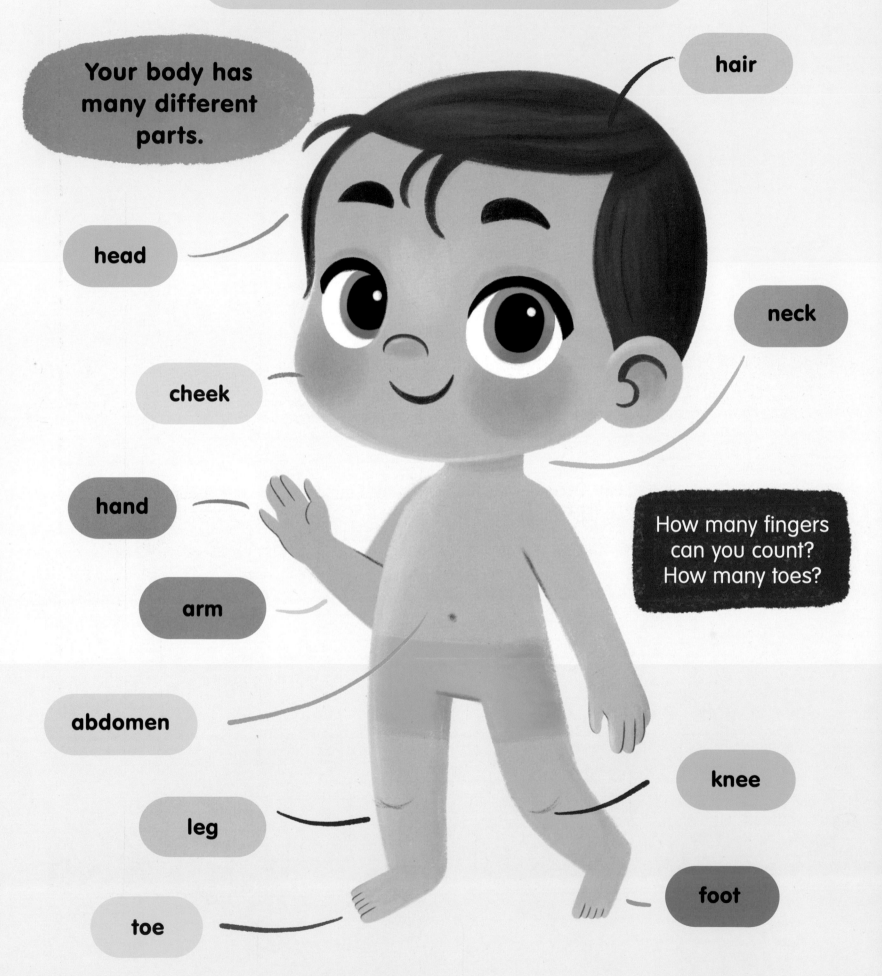

Your body has many different parts.

hair

head

neck

cheek

hand

How many fingers can you count? How many toes?

arm

abdomen

knee

leg

foot

toe

MAIN INTERNAL ORGANS

Brain

The brain tells your other body parts what to do.

Heart

The heart pumps blood all around your body.

Lungs

Lungs help you breathe. Take a deep breath in and let it out. You breathe in oxygen and breathe out carbon dioxide.

Small and Large Intestines

The intestines also help digest food and get rid of waste.

Stomach

The stomach helps you digest food.

YOUR FACE

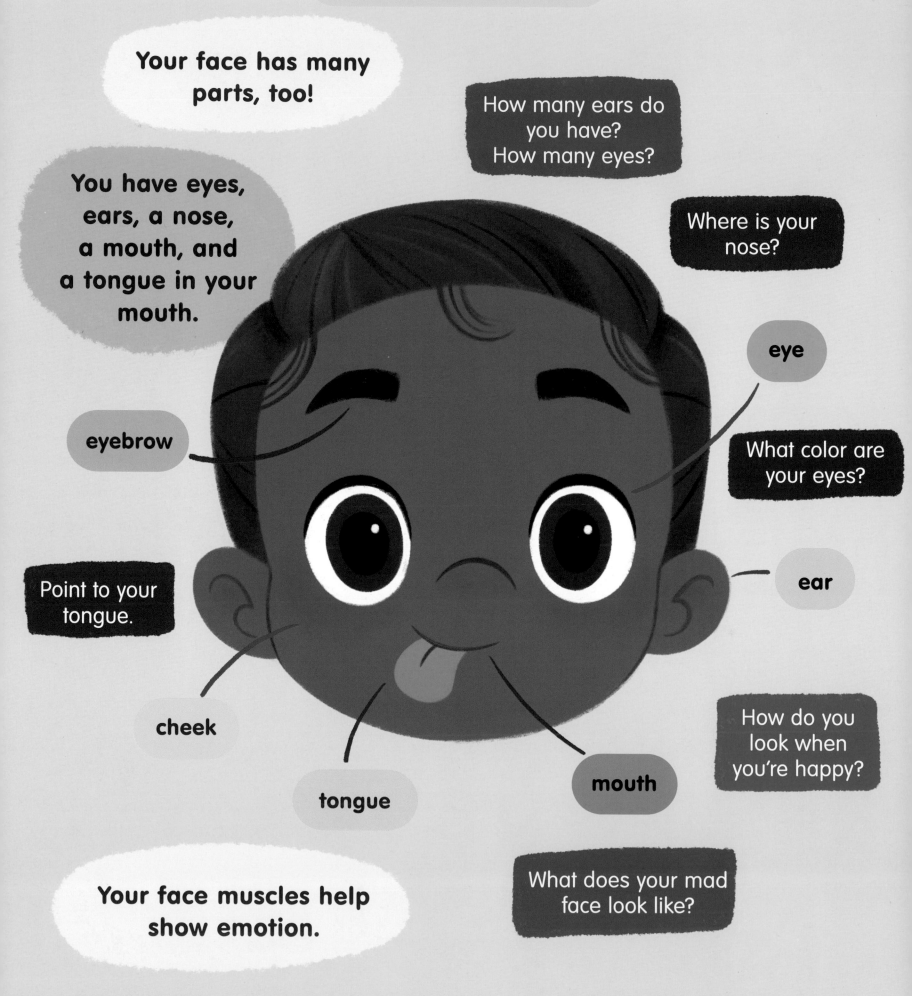

Your face has many parts, too!

How many ears do you have?
How many eyes?

You have eyes, ears, a nose, a mouth, and a tongue in your mouth.

Where is your nose?

eye

eyebrow

What color are your eyes?

Point to your tongue.

ear

cheek

How do you look when you're happy?

mouth

tongue

Your face muscles help show emotion.

What does your mad face look like?

SENSE ORGANS

smell

You smell with your **nose**.

hear

You hear with your **ears**.

see

Eyes can be brown, blue, hazel, gray, amber, or green.

You see with your **eyes**.

taste

You taste foods with your **tongue**.

touch

You use your **hands** to touch things.

BRAIN AND NERVOUS SYSTEM

Your brain tells your body what to do!
It has several parts that have different jobs.

Frontal lobe
This part helps you speak, have feelings, and remember things.

Parietal lobe
This part helps you detect pain, cold, and heat.

Occipital lobe
This part helps you understand things that you see.

Temporal lobe
This part helps you understand things that you hear.

Cerebellum
This part helps you move and balance.

Brain stem

Your brain has two sides. The left side controls what the right side of your body does, while the right side of your brain controls your left side.

CIRCULATORY SYSTEM

Your heart pumps blood to the organs in your body. Your organs need blood to work the right way.

When you're running, your heart beats faster. When you're sitting or sleeping, your heart slows down.

Place your hand on the left side of your chest. Can you feel your heartbeat?

HAIR AND SKIN

Your skin is actually an organ! It's the largest organ in your body. You feel pain, heat, and cold with your skin. It helps keep your internal organs safe, too.

We all have different colored skin, but it does the same job for everyone!

You might see places on your skin that are a different color.

Mole

A mole is a small birthmark.

Freckle

A freckle is a small brown spot.

Vitiligo

A person with vitiligo has white spots on their skin.

Sunburn

This is skin that has turned red from being in the sun too long.

Birthmark

Birthmarks can be any color, size, or shape anywhere on the body.

Bruise

A bruise shows up when something hits your skin hard.

The hair on your head keeps your head warm and protects your skull. Just like eyes, hair comes in different colors.

Blond

Black

Brown

Red

Auburn

Chestnut

Gray

White

Hair can be straight, wavy, or curly.

People can lose their hair.

BONES AND MUSCLES

Your body is made up of a bone structure that is called a skeleton. It protects your organs and helps you stand up straight. You also have muscles, which let your body move.

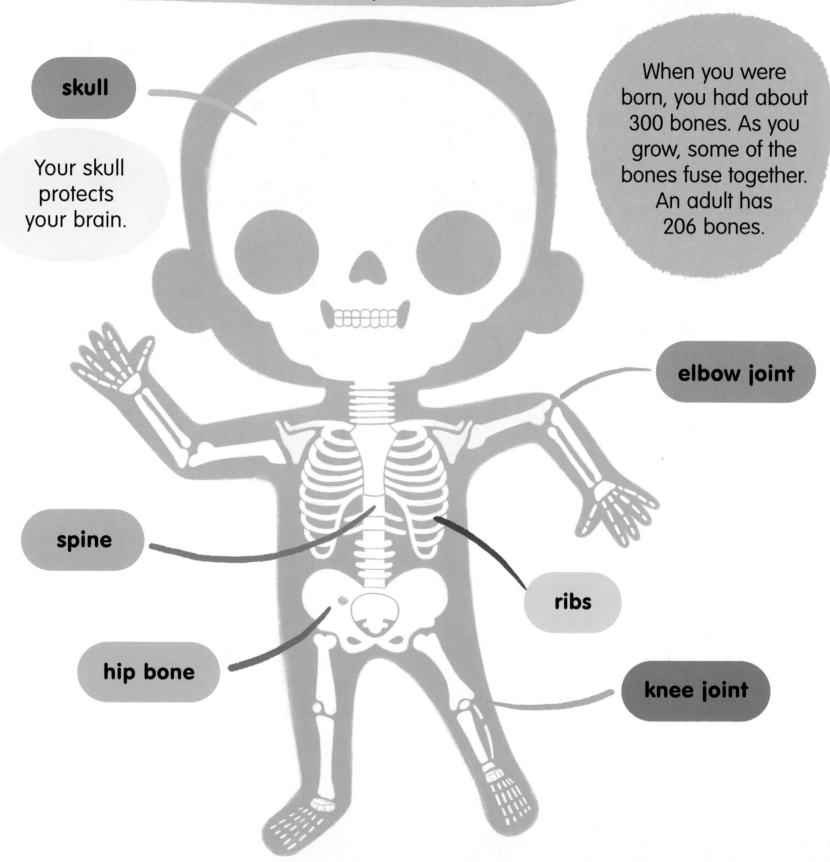

skull

Your skull protects your brain.

When you were born, you had about 300 bones. As you grow, some of the bones fuse together. An adult has 206 bones.

elbow joint

spine

ribs

hip bone

knee joint

Point to the taller person.
Point to the shorter person.

Sometimes, bones break.
Doctors use an X-ray
to see inside your body.

FOOT

Who has larger bones—the
woman or the boy? Where is the
person with big muscles?

Foods like milk, cheese,
fish, and broccoli help
keep your bones healthy.

5

Muscles can learn! If you do
something a lot, your muscles
remember what to do.

DIGESTIVE AND EXCRETORY SYSTEMS

Your digestive system helps your body use the foods you eat for energy.

Your excretory system gets rid of waste from your body.

esophagus

liver

stomach

small intestine

large intestine

You use your mouth to eat. Your teeth grind up food, and your tongue pushes the food into your throat. When you swallow, the food moves into your stomach.

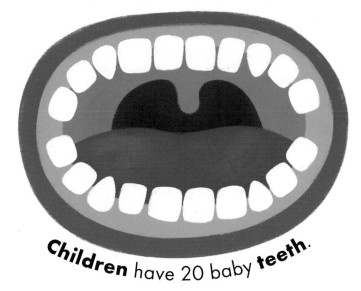

Children have 20 baby **teeth**.

When you're hungry, your **stomach** growls. Then your mouth fills up with **saliva**—the clear liquid in your mouth.

EXCRETORY SYSTEM

A clean mouth is a healthy mouth! Brush your teeth, use dental floss, and rinse with mouthwash twice a day.

kidney

bladder

Sometimes, your body doesn't need all the food you eat. The extra food travels into your small and large intestines. Then your body gets rid of the waste when you poop.

Your kidneys clean your blood. Urine (pee) stays in your bladder until you go to the bathroom.

STAYING HEALTHY

Germs are everywhere and can make you sick. Always **wash your hands** before and after you eat!

Wear **warm clothing** in the winter and whenever it's cold outside.

Exercise to have strong muscles and lots of energy.

Eat **healthy foods** to grow up strong and feel good.

Get your **shots** when it's time so that you don't get sick.

Get a good night's **sleep.**

GO TO THE DOCTOR FOR CHECKUPS

Doctors help us stay healthy! Make sure to see your doctor for regular checkups.

Where is the child who is having her eyes checked?

A dentist checks your teeth. Where is the dentist?

Do you see the doctor listening to the child's heartbeat?

Point to the child getting a shot.

YOUR BODY REVIEW!

You learned a lot about your body. Let's see what you remember!

Name each part of the body.

Point to the eyes.

Count the fingers on each hand.

Which organ can help you taste candy?

What part of your body do you use to feel a rough surface?

Which organ do you use to smell a flower?

This child has a sunburn. Which organ turned red?

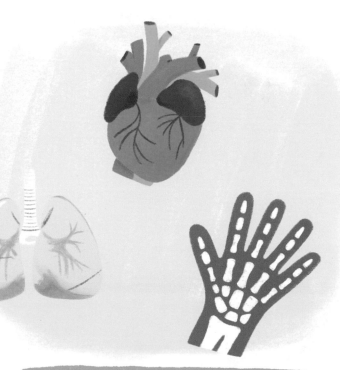

Which child feels cold?

A doctor can see inside your body using what kind of picture?

Which system moves blood around your body?